SEASONAL CALLS
(Poems)

AF528052

SEASONAL CALLS
(Poems)

Dr. Amita Saxena
Professor
College of Fisheries
G.B. Pant University of Agriculture & Technology
Pantnagar – 263 145, India

2011
REGENCY PUBLICATIONS
Delhi - 110 002

© 2010, AMITA SAXENA
ISBN 81-89233-67-X
ISBN 978-81-89233-67-9

All rights reserved, including the right to translate or to reproduce this book or parts thereof except for brief quotations in critical reviews.

Published by : **REGENCY PUBLICATIONS**
(*Division of Daya Publishing House*)
4760-61/23, Ansari Road, Darya Ganj,
New Delhi - 110 002
Phone: 23245578, 23244987
Fax: (011) 23260116
e-mail : info@regency-books.com
website : www.dayabooks.com
website : www.regencybooks.com

Laser Typesetting : **Classic Computer Services**
Delhi - 110 035

Printed at : **Chawla Offset Printers**
Delhi - 110 052

PRINTED IN INDIA

Contents

1. Sitting & Wishing 1
2. Eye Sparkle 2
3. Home is Rome 3
4. Control 4
5. You 5
6. No History 6
7. Motherland 7
8. Mirror 8
9. Heat Beat 9
10. Spring 10
11. Hill 11
12. Children 12
13. Life Effects 13
14. Evidence 14
15. Melody 15
16. India 16
17. A Sight 17
18. My Love 18

19. Father 19
20. Land 20
21. Song 21
22. Nature 22
23. Glimpse 23
24. Diamonds 24
25. Adversity 25
26. A Corpse 26
27. Life of Love 27
28. All Over 28
29. Not Mine 29
30. A Tree 30
31. The Conversation with God 31
32. The Day 32
33. Unseen 33
34. Thirsty Ocean 34
35. Way to God 35
36. Blessings 36
37. Limitations 37
38. A Word 38
39. Aim 39
40. Wake 40
41. The Bliss 41
42. My Fascination, Peacock 42
43. Feelings 43

44. Rains Rains 44
45. Waterfall 45
46. Come Again Rain 46
47. Snap Shots 47
48. Legend 48
49. Rakhi 49
50. Lunar Light 50
51. Gain 51
52. Think 52
53. A Hunt 53
54. My Dream World 54
55. My Father "Sun" 55
56. My Wings 56
57. A Fair in Town 58
58. Mobile 60
59. The Strength 62
60. Monsoon 63
61. Forest 64
62. Sea Wave 65
63. An Appeal (of Buffalo) 66
64. Dear Dog 67
65. Plantation 68
66. Cool, Cool 69
67. Green 70

Sitting & Wishing

One sitting on the bank,
Deep thoughts, wishes,
Reaching to its peak,
Of unknowing base, seek
But the wishes ……
Keep on sitting and wishing,
Oh my wishes come true or not,
Asking! Asking ……?
Bring back memory, passed time,
When I was bright,
Time passed, rusted me,
Torn me, turn me,
Still thinking …….greatness of others,
No person be great, sitting and wishing,
A fish treasures rivers have ……
Prepare the bait with specific ration,
Go on catching culture and fishing,
No way sitting and wishing

Eye Sparkle

Sparking alters lurid by
Sounds comes loudly,
Sparking, friction generate naturally
Same place, time, position, equally
Light reach fastly
Leaving all its, treasurally
As eyes sparkle naturally
Leaves aside ally
Reach to heart fastly
A sparkle is enough, lively

Home is Rome

Moving fast, loitering,
In a move, traveling,
Overshadow bluish sky,
Round, oval flat but gay,
Here, there, some where?
Thunder shower, splitted shower,
All like, children play,
Happy and gay,
Paddy fields flooding their way
Stinking in tanks, smell of water
Paper boats floating, straw, dust, planktons
Drifting, waving, sinking seeing all in tons
Muddy road, loudly women,
Passing umbrella over their head,
Sheltering tree, shops, shaped dome
Stopping rain, go their home,
Play their fame name now home is Rome.

Control

Sinking heart, withered rocks,
Sleeping eyes of the cocks,
Waiting fast, unbearable sleep,
Dream to leap .....
Tears flow, sky blow .....
Dreamings, coming, giving sorrow,
Weather, pleasant,
Eyes vacant,
Memory lingers,
It was kinders,
Wasting time, like a swine,
Control, control control,
You shall never be roll.

You

You easily recognized from others,
Able to fly, occur everywhere
Forests, grasslands, mountains marshes, waters
Adorned with colour beautifully
Flit among leaves, splash over water,
Most beautiful, most melodious, most admired you
Most difficult to imagine world without you.
Such as world without sunshine.
Soul move without mine, sunshine.
You ....

No History

I want to live on happy land,
Where there is no history, No record
Nobody knew what Napoleon, Elezabeth, Akbar, done
Monuments, record historian done
We are absorbed in problems of own,
When we read the history brand crown
We find
When they leave their foot prints on sand
We have no time, place to read them all
Didn't want to know, them all
Who was who, we only know, who is who

Motherland

Whole world is my motherland
All human beings are my sibling brand,
All enjoy as much freedom as I do,
Everyone shares in joys and sorrows of all mankind
Without any human inequality, kind
Let us work for this, this kind,
To make our dream come true,
Thinking become reality, true,
We all live with love, peace and gaiety, true.

Mirror

Looking at mirror
Reflecting face, as is the mirror,
Clear as clear I want,
Humorous, as humor, I want,
As the structure
Under microscope,
Umbrella telescope,
Broken mirror break my face,
Come down, move slightly
Oh what I see
It's my mirror
As new I am
So many mirrors in a mirror
So many face in a face of a mirror
Need to find it, where is it?
One can see as many faces as one wants
It was not only the face
But a reflection of life
As much as your life.

Heat Beat

Time passing so fast,
Not waiting the beat of heart vast,
Coordination gone away,
Cricket only to sway,
Sounding loud in their way
Emotions up and down to play
Struggling life nothing to lay
Time passing away
Heart beating away
Sentiments true going wild
Make every event wild
Heart with voice wild, life wild

Spring

In a crowded bus
From a window, I peeped
Splashing, fluttering, cluttering leaves
Countless, likely to be in corers
Dancing, singing
In a pleasurable romantic mood
I gazed the nature's wealth
I got refreshed health,
Mustard plants, canary yellow flowers
Grow and welcome the coming spring
Inviting us to go and join,
Thus, to treasure world of coin.

Hill

Sunny, on hill, melting snow,
Long fern, moss grow,
Temperature low, lips blue,
Hairy animals seeking warmth,
Freshy air, freshy face,
Tidy children moving fast, race,
Reached, destination, prayed welfare
Long upright trees, touching sky fare
Wooden house, fire place,
It is hill, live with grace.

Children

Children in a row,
Come and go, daily dew,
Weeping, sleeping but go,
Never forget their lunch box
Sometimes mischievous and cunning as clever fox
Making ladder, over their shoulder, jumping bladder,
Sometimes gesturing some time's
Miming, joining cadre
Talking loud while walking
Always coping, always coping
Doing the same as their elder do
Be good, do good, with them
To cause our generation good.

Life Effects

Great men always shine,
Nothing can effect, age or time,
Rain or Sun, shine,
Storm or cyclone,
Summer or winter,
Kindness or cruelty never wither,
Always remain the same,
What so ever the game,
Like a pillar, rock stands upright, fame,
Shelter others All on God's name.
Cruel Evil name,
On the God's name.

Evidence

Chirping birds, calling their mate,
Frogs extended their vocal sacs tartar,
Muddy water, flashing children,
Rusting leaves with pleasing breeze,
Ill will squeeze, going to freeze,
Blue of heaven seems clear
To its blooming blue
Giving me certain clue
Of your presence, somewhere perhaps here
Offerings near, near very near
Give evidences of you
Near, near and very near.

Melody

Melody of my suppressed tears
Heart, liver, brain drain tears
Costless tears withered eyes,
Causing, my soul dyes,
Comes out show them sorrow,
Perhaps I have to borrow
Peer fear, tear and only tear
Ocean dry, droughty area
Off water flood of my eye,
My instrumental water opens to sing,
Melody of my suppressed tears,
Coming up to sing my tears.

India

Beads scattered, collecting child
Guessing we are not wild
United heart, united mind
United eyes, united wind,
As rivers united to form ocean
Creating things, united us
Conquer the enemy, ignited us
Live long us, within precious India
Live long country–India

A Sight

River Ganges, flowing, reached Rishikesh,
Throwing Amrit all the way,
Every summer, it dries up
Watergates entangles, with straw sway
One can see bars of sand
Under the great hanging bridge
Black buffaloes lounging there
Away from the shining sunny stroke
Shining back, sitting crow,
We were standing in a row
Watching the lovely sight,
Of Mahaseer, Devi bright,
Or peaks of hill from right.

My Love

Soft and gentle, delicate pink face,
The subtle fragrance of you,
You as current as time,
Gives a fresh beautiful, irresistible feeling, forced
To meet the challenges of the future coarsed
This proof enough for your goof,
High standing in far dense dew, drops....

Father

The time I remembered when,
I was ill in the childhood, then,
Always care of me look by you father
Stories, comics, songs
Used to tell me, always busy with me
Now I have pain
But my father is no more
This doubles my pain.

Land

All the land are same,
Every child play the game,
Go and come outside the country,
But it is the native land,
Where, I want to live and die,
Away from cry and dry of temper
Alone with my fellow beings, pamper
With my own customs and traditions
In my beloved country India
Live, live for Ever
If I re-born
Born here
Serve here
For the cause of mankind
Oh! my beloved country India.

Song

Song for ceremonial occasion
Long as life ocean of passion
Harmonious as lively fashion,
Separating me from world of action,
As nuclear fission,
But still no mission,
To say, same,
Song for ceremonial occasion

Nature

Moving round and round the needle screw
Thinking, the passion grew
Bounded brain into pseudo vertigos
Trembling legs, increased heart rthyms
Away from the greatest feast of world,
The greatest pleasure of the world,
Where, when, how to measure, world
What is that treasure of Nature world,
Provide to each of us naturally,
By Nature's, Nature, Naturally.

Glimpse

I have seen you?
But never seen you actually
Things come to me naturally,
A blurred glimpse of you
Always remained with me,
Always remind, me
No body, seen you,
I waited for the day,
When a clear picture will appear of you,
Which will be stable as you!
When you stand and speak
In front of me.

Diamonds

Today, show yourself,
The time has come,
Nothing to worry,
Nothing to feel sorry,
No one is there,
Diamonds are there,
Pick up one by one,
Posture has come
Take them alone
You are alone.

Adversity

Life has stagnated,
All the zeal, enthusiasm spoiled,
Adversity over shadowed, mind,
Hopes are crushed, by favoritism
Empty heart, empty mind,
Everything lost nothing to find,
Loosened wishes shaking body,
Like a deep slept soul
Awaken naturally or artificially,
How?
But when and when? How?
I don't know, Now!

A Corpse

Like a floating corpse,
Though above the rich wealth of terrific sea
Under the magnificent sky,
Fearless moving fast dry,
Traveling on unknown path,
Nothing to wrath,
But waving for eternal world,
Where every thing is costless,
Going to be selfless.

Life of Love

The hill of death and destruction,
When fish away from the water
The penetrating eyes of vulture to eat the fish in gutter,
Shrill cry of mentals and orphans,
Accelerate the oscillations of my heart waves
To do, something against this tilt, saves
Change the tilt towards love and affection, flaxy,
Like deepest ocean brightest star in Galaxy.

All Over

Writing poem all over night,
My loving heart, singing all over night,
To make it bright,
To put the thing right,
Singing all over night,
Like coocko on mango's tree,
Like children when they free,
Like light during morning,
Like prince when he is crowning,
My loving heart singing all over night
The song of love, peace and amity
Close to all knitted tightly,
Singing poem all over night
To tell you the message so,
The song of love, affection and amity

Not Mine

Never wound that loves you
Never cause that loves you
Its grievous pain
For such a wound leading to in vain never heal
It ever heal
It creat the soul bound,
It will creat an other round
It will a negative sound
Not mine without any ground.

A Tree

Tree is one, serve the one?
You are one, do for one,
Give the protection,
For generous interaction,
It will give you the best,
At the time of rest,
New, there is no guest,
It will be the greatest fest,
Plant it and enchant it,
As it will grow,
Balance beauty, benefits will blow,
And your life will glow,
For which to writing the eternal flow.

The Conversation with God

When no body, with you,
Say to God.....
When nothing, to be done,
Say to God.....
You are alone, Say to God.
Your, torture, tension, tyranny are none,
You are the sun,
It was only their fun
You are my son
It is your dawn
Yes, its your crown
I have given to you
Without a frawn,
What you want
What is wrong
Say to God.....

The Day

The day has come,
In the public presence,
Put me on the way,
To be happy and gay,
Say me, you are my child,
Domesticated or wild
Every organism small or big
Bless you with regarded reward twig
They will do what you want,
You will do what I want,
I am you, you are me,
They should know what I mean,
I am the fate, closing their gate,
Why to sorry why to sorry
Why to worry.......
You are my crown oh my child,
As you are known,
I am with you,
I am in you.

Unseen

I have seen you,
So many tunes you,
Say many times,
But still unseen,
It seems to mean,
You would be
Better than,
As I deem
You are desire of me
Known to me
With your unknown name
I have seen you,
In my day dream.

Thirsty Ocean

The water of thirsty ocean,
Limited to drawing eyes,
Song of silence limited to throat,
Body of floating goat,
Desire of a mussel to form pearl,
Desire of barren desert swit
Would thunder shower curl
We, the water of thirsty ocean
With high tides of limitless desires,
Welcoming all in a thirsty ocean.

Way to God

No use of praying, God, superficially,
When your heart, full of muddy dirt,
Religious books are open in front of you
Tongue, eyes, body are not with you
Abuse, misuse others, repeating history,
Degraded harmory trust to mistry,
All right soul and spirit both
Entangled wants,
Is it concentration? No
Worship? No
A mechanical action of brain or routine, yes
It is superficial, despite of excessive deep chess
Open holy pages, open eye, flow
Over thought of world, Away from myth
Pray to God
God to God
Go with God.

Blessings

Oh! God bestow the blessing,
My soul is wishing,
Life is waiting,
Treasures are barren.....
Plough, irrigate, fertile them,
So, I plough, irrigate fertile my fellow beings,
Make our land to your land
Convert this dark band to bright broad band.

Limitations

Life is limited,
Things are limitless,
Time is limited,
Pleasure are limitless,
Loss or gain in life
Recognition of
Select one,
Make the limited... unlimited

A Word

My tongue tiedness,
Choked throat,
Unsigned song of silence,
Eyes opened wide,
Your eyes are guide,
Tell me how to say?
The unuttered words, Till now.....
The words you are waiting
Tune is waiting
Anxious to listen, environment.....
The words shining of ornament,
Who will say when,
I and you both are,
Tongue tied,
Then ......
Words come from eye
Do not be shy

Aim

I traveled without any definite aim,
I have knocked about the world a good deal name,
Will you go and see who is knocking at the door game
Opportunity?
Like a bidder in an auction by a stroke of hammer
Wake up, prepare, go avail, win win...... drummer,
By hitting, knock out at once
Until he exhausted
Aware aware, you are there
Ah! very much there.

Wake

I am beyond you range of thought even
I am indecisive to any kind of your doing
The so called matter, begin person called
Me immature, as you have not sign of maturity
Talking the positive,
Giving the negative,
Saying the negative,
To put you in trouble,
To pull out from trouble
Sowing weeds for you
Showing seed to all and you
Wake! Wake!
Watch ways!
Wicked persons
Wicked ways
Dont' believe
What they say.

The Bliss

I can understand you, the thoughts and feelings,
You can understand me, thoughts and feelings,
Doing, deedful dealings,
No one feeling what we dealing,
They are stones or the bones,
They never respire, never inspire, to tones
But they sounds loud
In enormous crowd
Sparking but darting,
Always.....
Doing dreadful dealings
What we do?
Shut the mouth
Keep quiet, what is wanting
Leave the doubts
Let them think, get a blissful think.

My Fascination, Peacock

While going home
I peep from earth to dome,
I give a refreshing pleasurable time to my eye,
Oh crowded bus, I say good bye,
Here, I and all gregarious peacock,
Seeing each other, round the clock,
Waiting for rains,
With sunny pains,
Moving to water vicinity,
Flying to touch the eternity,
When they dance will all endures,
Ways to enchant to find famous glore,
Oh! my fascination, I screamed,
Oh! my beloved dreamed,
I shall make a rain, chambered aviary,
Rains will come without a danger,
You will dance, your progeny enhance,
In a beautiful, rain reserve forest,
I will be under your charm arrest,
When I will be build the nest
Come to you and take the rest

Feelings

When you glide, tell me,
I put my slide, on you
To get you, wherever, you are,
Not allow any one to take your place
Where you are,
You want to go some another way,
I want you, to be, in a simple way
When, your roots reach my way
Heart, will free to its nurturing nutrients,
In water which will waiting, capture the caps
What you feel I know it?
What I feel you don't know?
When you know, time will go?
Time is very preciously precious,
This fact rely realize graciously, gracious.

Rains Rains

Rains Rains,
Give me sense of gain,
To dance with peacock,
Make me close to peacock,
Who dances for me,
Waiting for me,
Who does not know, my ways
Whose ways to swim,
Wings to start swim,
Which does not want
Come to original in this coming rains
Dance dance, see me, my mains
To see the world,
Soon soon, in this rain,
Rains come and peacock dances
Rainbow came repeated chances.

Waterfall

Rains Rains come again,
Let the peacock dance,
Love feather chance,
Let the fish breeds,
Farmer sow seeds,
Feeling of creatures,
Dealing with creatures,
Dancing with world,
Heart haunt with world,
Birds chant with sing,
Let them do what ever they sing,
Don't shout with thunder shower,
See singing bird's laughter lost lower,
Washing whether with whip,
Blowing birds with wet feather,
Beautiful birds flowing floods,
Floods taking hots, lots
Flowing water all over,
Water, water all over,
Stopping swimming worldly ways
Far from flying, fraying, foaming, furry days.

Come Again Rain

No body knows when it stops,
Cleaning the way, disaster stops,
Make us happy,
Plants to clean,
Allow us out of gloom
Animal to bloom
Fertile the soil,
Earth to boil
Make us happy
Till the time, we live,
Make us happy,
Thirsty desire,
To say come again and again
Tentalizing tingling rain
Once again......
Again, again and
Again

Snap Shots

Your thought occupy, my mind all the time,
Yes, no areana of conflicts
Creeps together all the time
Your eyes remains in my eyes,
Confirm confidence, constant, convecture,
Snap shots sings soft subdue slow,
Tell truth, lies together,
Most movement moves me, miss me, mingler
Laughter love lusty livelihood,
Warm weakness wonder falls
Broken beautiful bestow blessings balls
For all and all.

Legend

Am I feel?
Why people feel a broad harbour in my mind,
They rest and go for, various destruction kind,
I nuture them, believe of mine,
They flourish and say to mine,
They put me in dirty mind,
I collar them for their shine,
They call me mad,
These are bad,
Call of heart say to trine,
Cheers, couple cups say to wine,
Destroy the game, name and fame,
Do we can who failed when renamed,
A Legend, life once felt bright,
Shine in bright.

Rakhi

Rakhi all over the shops bazaar
Silken thread clipped with gold and silver color
Sister tied around wrist of her brother
Both feasting sweet, seeing each other
Blessing loving, kissing praying
Doing each year remember register to
Deligating help, care, protection human
See the faith lie of happy bands
Lovely hands by lovely hands.
N o w ....
Nature, world scenario have change
Not only brother, tie it to person of range.

Lunar Light

The journey of golden carp
In troughs, full moon light facing full shining silvery
Its willful powerful lithe body darting
Solid gold liquify floating on water surface
Gleaming gloriously, amazing lunar energy
Showing more than rejuvenate, reconserve energy
Giving realms of prosperity
In most powerful determination
Sheltered, protected with armored scales,
Accompanying with endangered Devi scales,
Begin to visualize the amazing change,
Flow sparkling, vibrant against the current
Bold beautifully bring a golden waterfall
Cascading over life for fortune fall.

Gain

Seeing me vulnerable alone
Seeing indecisive alone
The so called mature person called me immature
Spoling me
Kept me separate
Playing all notorious game
Killing me with full tame
Losing my name and fame
No body knows culprit in chain
It is not his gain
It is yours gain
Remember,
They are in
Your frame
It is your gain.

Think

I can understand your thoughts feelings
You can understand my thought feelings
Doing, deedful dealings
No one feeling what we dealing
They are stones or they are bones
They never respire, never inspire
But they sounds loud
In enormous crow
Sparking but darling
Always
Doing dreadful dealing
What we do...?
Shut the mouth
Keep quiet, what is wanting
Leave the doubts
Let them think, Get a blissful link

A Hunt

In this concrete world
In a hunt of honey dew,
Who pretends perhaps water of snow
Or my idleness eyes dew,
Sometimes, I felt in an airy crew,
Restless world sow me, watching few,
I have not seen, since I grew
This fascinating rift, make me swift
Catch a flower and swim with butterfly
Fly high, highest to the sky
Without typhoon, cyclone, Laila storm
I swarm surrounds my honey dew
Still hunt to conserve and hunt again
So long way to know hunt
And see my honey dew.

My Dream World

My dream world never come to me
I reached to that world, never
No way I think about
No way to meet about
But, I think to meet
My fires, feathers
Peak pleats flares
To open, to think
The world, way of mine
Shifting soul saying soft
Hoping hue, hopping happy
Live life, live in love
Swimming sky,
Strengthen strongest strong sea
Saw my sweeping soul
Thawing my calm from my
Coolest chill thy.

My Father "Sun"

See the sun
You are there
This is rare
You cannot compare
Yah! It is true
All above your dream
Jupiter says I am guiding you
Sun says I am shining you
Mars is protecting you
Moon says I am cooling you
You are sun
No body can displace or replace you
We all are with you.

My Wings

Whenever I see through the mountain
Pleasing cool sun, smile some special say,
Rainbow in stream, spirit, sea, summing sky
Rings in high heaven.....
Peaks purple blue seven.....
Picks colours from sun rays
Without burning bays
Or fire frays
Soul stars shine to sun
Who make my golden wings to
Radiant red,
Round and round, opened, round and round
Rings of rings
Crimson red, golden wings
Soaking me wet thick wings
With wired wings
I live, with heavy, stormy wings.....

Solar shine spread, high tide height
My wings flight
Stars see me, my desires
When I live long with fire
Sleep on sound fire
Sun at set says, I cannot rest in deepest ocean,
Same, I burned to ash to reach the deepest ocean.

A Fair in Town

In an occasional fair
In a lot of fun, no one can imaginer
Whey you stood aside in medieval panes
Story tellers wander all the ways to lanes
Songs with actions as heroes of bottles ward
Gypsy dancers shimmered through crowd
Goody, twist, twirl to drum focussed beat
Man on motor bike whirling in blind well
Moving motion circulating cell
Many swings, Mary gold round
Fast track train, Top wheel, Draggers, Oscillators
Furniture stall, sit a while fragrance comes
Shops of cloth, crafts, decors, flowers, jewellery,
  carpet, chat, churan, chutney tastes
Fashion show, baby show, music nights
Flame tossed noodles
Oh! deliciously baked scented smell.....

Omelet potato bread, *Halwa parantha* smell
Enhance entertainment of hours
Enjoy time, take a break
Feel free from all the bond
Join someone or group for
Joint endeavor
Be a leader
Show the fair
Shift in your behavior
Don't be in profound thought
Donate some charity
Be in complete flexibility
Be stimulated this way in fair
Promote your success in big way fair.

Mobile

Mobile make me docile
Restrict me into immobile
I lost you so many times
I do not know where are you
And to whom with you
You are no chat with someone
And with me on mobile
You cut me from real world
And on top of the waves world
Waves of mobile, not of you
My passion becomes yours passion for chat
With someone, I do not know, speakers on.....
You sometimes put me in craves cave
No body knows your chat friend
How you exploit passion for another one
Today's mobile, TV, Internet
I came into net.

I am in the world but away from world
In communication without communication
Within the society
But away from the society
How unsocially, touching dreams
Away from truth
Dream inventions followed by?
Idle world, connecting others
I am alone, in electronic world.

The Strength

Great strength
Require great attention
Yes attention and care
Keep the flame burning
Inspiration of idyllic vision
To pour fresh energy emission
Burning urge quest
Shape the flame
Solemnly flaring fire power
Faming passion
Fulfilling intimidation
Revitalizing love magically
Sparkalise new life
Somatically chemical energy expresses
All ATPs reflect you
A great strength of me in you.

Monsoon

Monsoon ushers arrival,
Cause garden survival,
Partial monsoon, humid, warm day, wet soil
Reporting plants
Old leaf mould
Shall producing gold,
Balsam, photos, salvia, cosmos
Burrowing worms forming round on ground,
Creeping on roofs, sound proofs
Monsoon already come, collect........collect........collect...
Mooning mossy carpet all around.

Forest

Green leaves, long trees, thick forest,
Who refreshing refilling air, I know
Watched the dew on leaves, grasses, grow
Wild animals, wandering woo, boo, bees, freely
Wild environment all over, natural and daring, daily
Forced me to live these, without any fear,
The wind blow through tree, tyre,
Animal ready for sleep, alert me!,
And I recognize, much has yet to be done,
Having done nothing, even animals have done,
Cautioned! heart throbbed,
To fulfill duties to my fellow beings.

Sea Wave

The lovely, alluring, evening
Quiet, calm, free from pollutants, air daring,
Wide, round red Sun in blue bright sky,
Setting down in west after a long ride,
The pleasurable sea spring and leap tide,
Comes and goes, wetting the shore high and far,
Deep sensation of cold and peace and love,
Salty drips with edible organisms,
All eternal, penetrating heart to soul from skins,
Everlasting to every one,
No distinction of rich or poor able or disable,
Famed or defamed, child or old,
Clean or dirt, stone or gold
Do its eternal duty to all, hot or cold.

An Appeal (of Buffalo)

My senses stretched,
My tissues crushed,
Nerves reach to its, long last tension,
When I get my due pension?
Injuries on buffalo body ....
Fly fleas infecting, wounded, body .....
No body bothers my (buffalo) cuts and tears, tyres
Seasonal cloth you can wear,
Only language, I have to bear,
Have you seen my food, space, shelter
Am l, a defaulter ?
Why you become, so cruel .....
Despite doing duties dual,
Let you make more trips,
Half the language, half the whip,
When I lie, you will cry, I will die cause, you dry
Become, a man
Let me live
For you and myself.

Dear Dog

Discipline Master
Disciplined Dog black feathery silky,
Soft shampooed hair come to car,
Sat on seat
Never moved peeping from window
Only slippery seats, unstable feet fearful eyes
Car stopped,
Change the mood,
Come down from car
Comfortable walk, seeking ground or waiting
I called upon him/see it
Jumped cried lick, the feet
Moved with disciplined master
Forget car, company call
Master's movements, meeting me
My master, my master, meeting me

Plantation

Keep your things clean and green,
May be forest, lake, river or a foreseen,
As you share space, floor, food, freedom and water,
And happy with your beloved pretty pets & daughter,
When you give precious breed,
Breed will give you better seed,
Sow these seeds not the weed
This will be the world's greatest pleasure
And never ending Nature's greatest pleasure
Remember they will fulfill all your need
But not the greed, Do this deed

Cool, Cool

October is going with wind of hope,
Winter is coming with way of hope,
Though the water freeze,
Many million organisms do or die
Vegetations flame frost, fume
But the human beings are happy, of coolness,
Just the atmosphere, give him happiness, calmness
Why not you.............
You are a person, to be good
Give goodness to all
Give cooling, soothing effect to all
By only yours cool temperament
This would be a best tournament.

Green

Plants are green,
Green is the garden,
Make your heart garden,
Be green, do green
And live with green
Because green is always green,
Prosperous, gorgeous where and when
Prosperity and goodness to all others
Bridge the breaches, and beeches
Otherwise, will breach the bridges.

S.B. 25/5/06 - 5085

Serial-32
16/5/06